THE SCIENCE
OF CO-CREATION

THE SCIENCE OF CO-CREATION

A Maha way to Manifest Your Desires

Sunil Chhaya

PARTRIDGE

To order additional copies of this book, contact
Partridge India
000 800 919 0634 (Call Free)
+91 000 80091 90634 (Outside India)
orders.india@partridgepublishing.com

www.partridgepublishing.com/india

"Gayatri Mantra"

**"OM BUHR, BHUVA, SWAHA
OM TAT SA VITUR VARENYAM
BHARGO DEVASYA DHEEMAHI
DHIYO YONAHA PRACHODAYAT"**

(We meditate on the glory of the Creator;
Who has created the Universe;
Who is worthy of Worship;
Who is the embodiment of Knowledge and Light;
Who is the remover of Sin and Ignorance;
May He open our hearts and enlighten our Intellect).

CONTENTS

I   **ALCHEMIST'S VIEW** 1

    i) Our Universe 1

    ii) Energy fields of the Universe 1

    iii) The Cycle of Elements: 3

    iv) The Human..6

II   **MAHAVASTU A SCIENCE** **11**

    i) Concept 11

    ii) Zones and their significance...............................13

III **GOVERNING UNIVERSAL LAWS** **19**

    i. The Law of Attraction 21

    ii. The Law of Deliberate Creation...........................25

    iii. The Law of Sufficiency and Abundance.................27

    iv. The Law of Pure Potentiality:- 35

    v. The Law of Detachment:- 37

    vi. The Law of Polarity:- 40

    vii. The Law of Reflection:- 44

    viii. The Law of Forgiveness:-................................47

    ix. The Law of Gratitude:- 49

IV **HUMAN MIND - Limiting Beliefs and Mental Blocks** 53

V Expand and Evolve the Universe.. **59**

   i - Directions and Placements:-..59

   ii - Science of Programming and Connecting
to the Source Energy 62

   iii - Manifestation 68

VI CO-CREATION EFFECT OF MAHAVASTU **75**

Foreword

Awareness about the power of your Inner Mind has been on the rise these days. It is only recently that people have started talking more about the hidden power of the Subconscious Mind and Positive Thinking.

One, who has learnt to tame his mind can get magical and unbelievable results in no time. Those who are new to Law of Attraction may not believe it but let me tell you that the universe is catching the frequency of your thoughts every minute and every second and you are going to get surprising results from your own thoughts. Whatever you are thinking right now, is going to come back to you. The Law of Attraction believes in the process of 'like attracts like'. If you are having good and positive thoughts, you will attract back positive and happy circumstances and events in your life. The universe around you is receiving signals from you and sending back the same emotions.

Similarly, MahaVastu, the modern version of Indian science of Vastu teaches the techniques on how to unleash the powers of your subconscious mind. After a two-decade study on effects of surroundings and built up spaces on human behaviour, I have discovered that mind is the most powerful search engine. Your mind reflects what you think. It never works on its own. It's your thoughts, which make it work. The phenomenon of the mind exists at three levels: The first level is the individual mind, the second is the Space where a person lives and the third is the Universal Mind.

After discovering this truth, I understood that Space around keeps on sending signals to the universe. So, if the Space is programmed according to your wishes, you can attract wealth, growth, love, happiness, health and whatever you desire. For the Programming of the Space, we developed many Remedies. These remedies activate the Universal Energies to generate special powers and these powers lead us towards the achievement of your goals and desires.

By writing 'The Science of Co-Creation - A Maha way to Manifest Your Desires', Sunil Chhaya has done a commendable job. He has combined two sciences together and created a piece of life changing literature. This book fills currently unmet need for a real, practical and scientific analysis of human mind and need to generate positive behaviour, which I am sure, if understood and used by humans can create magical differences in their lives.

It is evident that the book is essential for attracting Money, Health, Love and Happiness. I am gratified with the work of Sunil and congratulate him for creating a Master Product while balancing the Science of Vastu and Law of Attraction.

Khushdeep Bansal

Founder MahaVastu and Author of world's biggest book on Vastu Shastra- "MahaVastu Handbook"

Inspiration

KB sir:- My utmost Gratitude to my mentor and My Guru, VastuShastri Dr. Khushdeep Bansal, founder of Maha Vastu liked to be called "KB". His belief in me and guidance on the basic concepts of the 12000 years old Indian Science "The Alchemy of Space" called Vastu Shastra, which he has now made it known as "MahaVastu". The Science of Programming your Space be it the Inner Space, the Space you live in or the Outer Space -The Universal Space.

This programming tames your sub-conscious mind to deliver results that you want to reach. A Miracle that you see happening in your everyday life.

KB with his family of MahaVastu Experts are reaching to mankind from all walks of life across the globe to help them "Tame their Universe".

My special thanks to all of the Maha Vastu family and especially Shri Nitin Guptaji and Ms. Silky Rainaji who has been instrumental in coordinating and putting in a conscientious effort with all concerned to bring a fruitful and legally correct version of my book.

My heartfelt thanks with appreciation to

Shaz and Shiraz Golden Inspirations:- The people and the organisation who taught me the ABC of Law of Attraction and trained me to train others use the of Law of Attraction. I, remain ever so obliged to the whole team of Golden Inspirations, India.

Christy Whitman, The lady behind the most disciplined, Enthusiastic and Energetic coaching academy for creating Success and Life coaches for showing way to people for living the life they want, in her academy, known as "The Quantum Success Coaching Academy,(The QSCA) USA."

They teach us how to coach and assist people in Deliberately using The laws of the Universe in everyday life and to achieve the desires and goals. I am and will always remain obligated to her.

Esther Hicks and Jerry Hicks for their processes of Abraham, in their awesome book "Ask and it's Given".

Rhonda Bryne the author of the book and the film "The Secret" which has taken the world by storm and shown to the world the very secretly and suppressed for centuries, "The law of Attraction".

My wife Tripti, an ever so busy professional singer in Gujarati, who travels round the globe spreading "the Indian culture and it's teachings" to apply in one's life and enhance the quality of life. My sons Deep, Nishad and their better-halves, Soumya and Deepa and ofcourse my two little grandchildren, Shivank and Eira for giving me the impetus to write this book. And all my family members who cooperated with me for giving birth to this book.

My friend Ghanshyam Paranjape, whose guidance helped me tremendously in the technicalities of making the document on the computer and the brainstorming sessions for writing and successfully accomplishing completion of this book.

My editors, publishers, legal advisors, designers, "The Partridge Publishing Company, India, for designing and bringing forth the instant cover page and the fotos and concept of QR codes into this book.

INTRODUCTION

In the process of Evolution, unless something is manifested, the universe does not expand. However, we all know that the Universe is ever expanding and evolving. So it is obvious that manifestation is taking place all the time. This manifestation by us humans is either by default, that is unknowingly, be it good or bad, or by deliberately creating whatever that is required to fulfil one's desires, goals, passions which in effect is assisting the universe to expand and evolve, by virtue of giving something to someone when it is right for that person.

This deliberate manifestation is called co-creation and making use of the process in a scientific and logical manner is thus called,

"The Science of Co-Creation".

I

ALCHEMIST'S VIEW

i) Our Universe

Our Universe comprises of all existing Matter and Space as a whole.

The Universe is believed to be at least ten billion light years in diameter and contains innumerable Galaxies. It is ever-expanding and evolving since its creation in the Big Bang Theory, some billions of years ago.

"Give Joy and Abundance to the world, share and show the way for Growing Our Universe".

ii) Energy fields of the Universe

We are all surrounded and Governed by energies of which not much is known. There exists such energies which we neither know they exist nor do we know anything about these energies. Human conscious mind has just about 2% of knowledge of these, and these energies are the ones that govern our every aspect of life. They are known as

1

the Universal energies. They influence our very existence. Researchers have found that there are about 24 Universal energies governing us.

However, in our Indian Vedic strictures, it is said that there are in all 1024 Universal energies and that they are represented by the 1024 Lotus petals on the Crown Chakra (Shahshar Chakra) located about six inches above our head. (incidentally it is 10th order of 2 i.e. 2^{10}, which is also the base in our current computer world) Out of these only 45 energies are useful for governing our existence. Each petal controls one attribute, such as blinking of our eyes, our breathing, heart beats, functioning of involuntary organs, the Hypothalamus glands, to name a few.

These 45 energies attribute to different functions of the body, it's Creativity, Spirituality, Health, Healing, Intuition, Abundance and also Anxiety, Stress, Failure, Negativity, Diseases, anti-social behaviours and so on. All these energies are created one by one in the liveable space from the time it's construction commences. Step by step they develop in a volumetric manner. They consist of self-illuminating as well as negative energies which locate themselves in a specific manner and location as a conglomeration of different energy fields with the resultant energy at the outermost core of the space determining the control of a different aspect that govern our life and thereby our existence.

iii) The Cycle of Elements:

All of existence whether physical or energies have been created with five natural elements namely, Water, Air/ Wood, Fire, Earth and Space.

This can be explained in the form of three main cycles:-

a) The Cycle of Creation (Brahma - The Creator - as in Hindu Mythology):

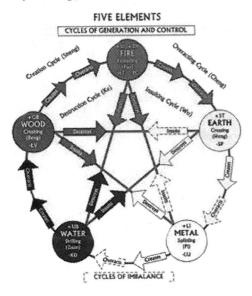

The cycle of creation is Water- creates Air/Wood - brings about Fire - which forms Earth and the Earth forms Space/Metal - This Space then forms Water and the cycle continues and happens from the macro to the micro level.

In the physical world, it's something like this:-

A flowing Thought (Spark/Water), leads to an Action (Karma/Air/Wood) which gives you a Result (Fire). This result gives Stability to one's life (Earth) and thereby a Status (Space) in life.

b) The Cycle of Control (Vishnu - The Maintainer):

This is when all the five elements are in their respective places and are helping each other to maintain the flow of energies. In balancing the creation of each element, the other four elements simultaneously influence and impose the control in following fashion.

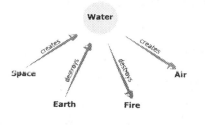

a) Water- It is created by Space, and itself creates Air /Wood, douses Fire and is held by Earth.

b) Air/Wood - It is created by Water, and itself creates Fire, tears the Earth and is cut by Space.

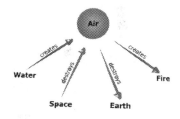

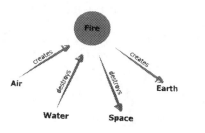

c) Fire - It is created by Air/Wood, and itself creates Earth, melts Space and is doused by Water.

d) Earth - It is created by Fire, and itself creates Space, holds Water and is torn by Air/Wood.

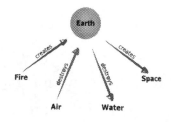

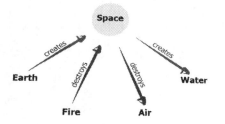

e) Space/Metal - It is created by Earth, and itself creates Water, cuts Air/Wood and is melted by Fire.

c) The Cycle of Destruction (Mahesh - The Destroyer):

The way these elements have the capacity to create, balance, they also have capacity to destroy. Here is how the destruction takes place as below:-

Water – Dowses *Fire*
Fire - Destroys *Space/Metal*
Space/Metals - Cuts *Air/Wood*
Air/Wood - Ruptures *Earth*
Earth – Holds *Water*

When all these five elements are in balance the mind becomes more receptive and sensitive to objects and activities in a space.

iv) The Human

The body consists of the Five Natural Elements and is made up of Earth element from hips and below, Water around the stomach region, Fire glowing in the stomach, Air from chest to the throat and Space from throat to the head. In fact every particle in the universe is created out of these five natural elements. The whole balance of the Universe is depending on the behaviour of these five elements. Let us see how this balance is maintained.

As explained above, Human body is made from these elements. The various energies created from the elements work on our body at different levels called layers or Koshas. The human body's capabilities to perform shows the level at which the person has evolved.

Let us take a glimpse of what is meant by layers or Koshas.

The Five Layers of Existence:-

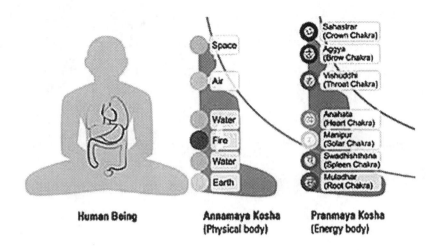

Very subtly speaking, our body consists of five layers starting from the Real You or the Physical part of You –This Physical body (Annamaya Kosh) is Nurtured and maintained by Food, Water, Air and the like.

The Energy body (Pranmaya Kosh) – Has the energy centres (Chakras) and meridians carrying energy around in our body. When you are in a Happy, Joyous and a 'Feeling Good' state of mind, you feel excited, high in energy, enthusiastic and desirous or having that spark within to do something good in life and live a purposeful life. When you are in a negative emotion, a bad feeling, your energy levels feel low and you are depressed, feel unwanted, useless, good for nothing type of state of mind.

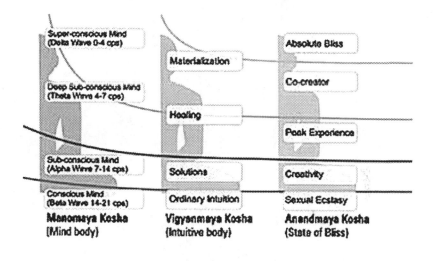

The Mind Body (Manomaya Kosha) - The Mind is also a body, and as described above, has different levels of activities, giving the respective benefits and purpose at each level.

The Knowledge body (Vigyanmaya Kosha) - Our Knowledge body, stores all the knowledge of this birth as well as previous births as part of evolution and at the right time and need imparts the required knowledge to create a experience, event, situation in a person's life. This body is connected to the most subtlest of them all, that is the Soul Body (Anandmaya Kosha). This is the Joy body or the body when one attains Absolute Bliss.

II

MAHAVASTU A SCIENCE

i) Concept

Humans created homes or shelters for their survival. Earlier there was a definitive science developed called Vastushastra wherein it was defined to locate various utilities of households to have beneficial effects of the various energy fields. In today's congested mega cities, it is not possible to create dwelling or accommodation based on the guidelines of Vastushastra, After years of research and thousands of case studies, a more Scientific and logical approach on the remedies of Vastu Shastra have been found by Vastushastri Dr. Khushdeep Bansal, which he preaches as 'MahaVastu'.

What do we understand by word 'MahaVastu'? MahaVastu is a science and we know that science is all about logical application of knowledge. The space in which we live, work or do any activities is governed by our sub-conscious mind and is known as the Inner Mind. The space outside any of these is called as the outer space and represents the Conscious Mind. The point at which you enter the inner space is known as the Connector. This connects you to the Universal space or better known as Universe. MahaVastu is a science that connects you with the Universe and aligns you with the flow of energies.

The MahaVastu solutions is a four-step method of programming the inner space to fulfil or achieve whatever that is you want to Be, Do or Have in your life. This science of programming becomes an intrinsic part of co-creating your desired life.

The first step is to find out what exactly is your priority of wants or desires.

The second step in MahaVastu is identifying the various zones which govern different aspects of our everyday life in relation with the layout of the liveable space. The positive and negative aspects that can be favourably used for a faster and effective solutions by positioning certain objects without making drastic changes to the existing utilities. As you will see in the figure below, the zonal aspects read in the clockwise manner, marked on the circle circumscribing the liveable space, there are pies representing sixteen different zones. All these aspects work together at different points in our life and affect our life. They are having both a positive effect and a negative effect depending on the activity/utility you are carrying out in that part of the liveable space. This you will understand clearly when you know the "where" as explained in the following third step.

The third step is to identify whether there are any existing anti-elements by way of shapes, colours, metals or anti-activities like toilets, kitchen, microwave ovens, mixers, washing machine, prayer area, mirror, storage, television, dining area, overhead water tank, underground tank, bore well and the like in places where it obstructs the aligning of your sub-conscious mind in your daily life and these match totally with the symptoms which seem to be hampering your life at that point of time. The sub-conscious mind as you know, is like a sponge and it absorbs anything and everything whether good or bad.

The Fourth step is about placements and relocation of activities and balancing all the five elements in the liveable space, to bring about the desired results.

ii) Zones and their significance

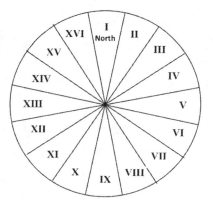

Zone I:- Zone of *Money and Opportunities*:-

This gives birth to your dreams and desires. The flowing energy increases and encourages the "spark" in you to passionately follow your dreams and desires. Opportunities are created and efforts are fruitful.

An ideal location for children's bedroom for enhancing their careers.

Zone II:- Zone of *Health and Immunity*:-

This brings balance between the Physical and Mental health. It boosts your immune system.

An ideal location for placing medicines, as it's effects get enhanced.

Zone III:- Zone of *Clarity and Mind*:-

This imparts Wisdom, Foresight, Intuition, Vision and Inspiration. Remove all unwanted and dead storage and keep the zone clean, neat and tidy as that reflects your mental and physical clarity.

An ideal zone for Meditation.

Zone IV:- Zone of *Fun and Recreation*:-

The energy here eliminates negativity and infuses positivity and vitality in the mind. It therefore governs fun and Recreation in life.

An ideal zone for a Family lounge.

Zone V:- Zone of *Social Associations*:-

Humans are social animals. To bring in more connectivity socially with fellow-beings, be it at home, work or play, This zone helps in building up of required cooperation.

An ideal location for a Drawing room.

Zone VI:- Zone of *Anxiety and Churning*:-

This zone imparts depth in the thought process and a deeper understanding of things. However, on the flipside it can make one, more anxious or argumentative.

An Ideal location for placing laundry or washing machine, a mixer or grinder.

Zone VII:- Zone of *Cash Liquidity and Fire*:-

This zone adds Zeal, Fire, Courage, and Vigour in life. The energy of this zone sustains the availability of Liquid cash.

An ideal location for placing cash counter, safe, lockers.

Zone VIII:- Zone of *Power and Confidence*:-

This zone brings in confidence and power over our decisions and actions. On the flipside, it lowers energy, bringing in lack of strength, stamina, vigour and vitality.

An ideal location for Kitchen.

Zone IX:- Zone of *Fame and Relaxation and Rest*;-

This zone revitalises and releases stress of body and mind. It is responsible for Fame and Social reputation in your life.

An ideal location for Master Bedroom.

Zone X:- Zone of *Disposal and Expenditure*:-

This zone rids one of all waste and useless things in life, however, if an activity like a bedroom is located in this zone then it gives rise to wastage of efforts for money resulting in unwanted expenditure, mounting debts, slow deterioration of health.

An ideal location for a Toilet.

Zone XI:- Zone of *Relationships and Skills*:-

This zone stabilizes family bonding, relationship, marriage of children, improves skills imbibed by our ancestors and brings out the dormant and latent talents.

An ideal location for displaying Certificates, Degrees, Rewards.

Zone XII:- Zone of *Education and Savings.*

This zone is of acquiring knowledge and education. It assists in increasing savings. Inspires performance and brings in greater returns with least efforts.

An ideal location for Study Room.

Zone XIII:- Zone of *Gains and Profits*:-

This zone gives Maximum returns, profits and gains expansion of business and minimum wastage on efforts put in. It is a life food for the body.

An ideal location for Dining room.

Zone XIV:- Zone of *Depression and Detoxification*:-

This zone helps in releasing stress and depression and helps to detoxify the body.

An ideal location for Spa or placing dust bins.

Zone XV:- Zone of *Support and Banking*:-

This zone is best for garnering active support from friends, relatives or any government authority. It also provides support from banks and Financial institutions.

An ideal location for Granary storage.

Zone XVI:- Zone of *Sex and Attraction*:-

This zone helps in deriving fulfilment and sensual enjoyment. Strengthens bond between spouses.

An ideal zone for newly married couple.

III

GOVERNING UNIVERSAL LAWS

As we know, Humans are in the continuous process of discovering various working principles of Universe. The branch of studies of these is called Physics and it is still evolving.

> What is Understood is *Physics*
>
> What is still being explored is *Quantum Physics*.
>
> What is not Understood is *Meta Physics*.

While studying and discovering Quantum Physics it is found out that, it is nothing but various unknown Rules/ Laws evolved by the Universe itself for the disciplined behaviour of the self. Whether you are aware of these governing laws or not, they are universally applicable. Just like the Law of Gravity, as said earlier, if you fall off a building, it does not matter, whether you are a good person or a bad person, you are going to hit the ground. These laws are followed by the universe which are now getting slowly known to humans, though the exact process involved is still a mystery however the end result is witnessed. Some of the known laws are mentioned under:

i.   Law of Attraction

ii.   Law of Deliberate creation.

iii. Law of Sufficiency and Abundance

iv.   Law of Pure Potentiality

v.   Law of Detachment

vi.   Law of Polarity

vii. Law of Reflection.

viii. Law of Forgiveness.

ix.   Law of Gratitude.

So let's begin our journey into the mysteries of our universe by understanding something about these laws.

i. The Law of Attraction

"We all work with one Infinite power, we all guide ourselves by exactly the same Laws. The Natural Laws of the Universe are so precise, that we don't even have difficulty in building a spaceship and send people to the moon and time the landing with the precision of a fraction of a second. I don't care if you are an Indian, if you are an Australian, New Zealand, or Stockholm or London, and Toronto or Montreal, or New York, we all work with one power, one law, it's Attraction, the secret is the 'Law of Attraction'."

—*Bob Proctor (The Secret).*

The most important and the Primordial Law is 'The Law of Attraction'. While manifesting, all the other Laws work in tandem to this Primordial Law. Just like the Law of Gravity, all these laws are working all the time on everything and on everyone, whether you know it, believe it, understand it, have faith in it or not.

What do you understand by the Law of Attraction?

Simply put:-

a) Thoughts Become Things.
b) That which you Focus upon Grows
c) Like Attracts Like.

Thoughts Become Things

Do you know how everything around us including everything here is built by dreamers. Everything before inception has been somebody's passion. Whether its a table, chair, laptop, this book or even a car, everything started with a thought initially.

What you Focus on, grows stronger in Life

When we decide to buy a car, we see the same car with the same colour everywhere. Law of Attraction in action.

Sometimes you are not sure which car you want to go for, however, you know for sure which car you definitely do not want to buy. In the process you don't make up your mind about the model but every time you repeat which model you do not want. When you are pressed for buying, invariably you will end up buying the car which you never wanted. This because the unwanted model remains in mind all the time and gets focused on.

Like Attracts Like

"Birds of same feather flock together", how all the studious students make their own group right on the first day of the school.

Everything in this universe is available in groups. Because similar things attract each other.

Coal is available only in coal mines, grass is available only in grasslands, sand dunes only in deserts and water from around the world tries to travel and merge into the ocean.

We attract whatever is there in our minds, whether it's something we want or something we do not want.

Just close your eyes and do not think of a black monkey. You will usually end up thinking about the black monkey.

Universe works exactly in this way, when we think of what we do not want, we get what we do not want in life.

Think of only those things you want in your life. Things you do not like, just don't think about them.

"This can be summed up in these three words: "Thoughts Become Things" - Mike Dooley (The Secret)

In short, Law of Attraction is applicable in our lives whether we know about it or not and whether we believe in it or not.

What we think/feel, we are bound to attract into our lives. So when you want to attract a certain thing in life, don't just think about it, FEEL it and Feel it with PASSION.

Nothing is impossible for Law of Attraction. Whatever you dare to think, you can achieve. How far we can go, is only limited by our thoughts.

Law of Attraction is not at all a new concept. Many a known people and more were aware about this law and have used it in their lives in one way or the other. This is proved from the works they did as the world knows of even today.

Plato - a Greek philosopher, as well as mathematician,

Music is a Moral Law, It gives Soul to the Universe, Wings to the Mind, Flight to Imagination and Charm and Gaeity to Life and to Everything.

Paramhans Yoganand – A direct disciple of Lahiri Mahasaya.

He introduced Kriya Yoga to millions of Westerners.

Albert Einstein – A Nobel prize winner in Physics,

The inventor of Theory of Relativity, said 'Thank-You' at every step he walked.

Napoleon Hill – A Famous Author

He wrote an all time best seller "Think and Grow Rich." Of which 20 million copies were sold. He quotes **"Whatever a Mind can Conceive and Believe, the mind can Achieve."**

Dale Carnegie – Motivational Speaker and Author.

"Happiness doesn't depend on any existing conditions, it is Governed by our Mental Attitude."

Emile Coue, who said these 'attracting' words:- *"Everyday in Every way I am feeling Better and Better."*

Try and say these yourselves, and you will be surprised to see how your body starts responding positively to these words. They have tremendous power.

ii. The Law of Deliberate Creation

The second Essential Universal Law is the Law of Deliberate Creation, and this is where the fun begins. You can use the Universe as a catalogue, just flip through the pages and ask for an experience, a soul mate, a good relationship, with feeling and great desire, and you get it. It's that easy, and once you have learned the art and skill of 'asking' the universe, you will realize the ease at which you can create your own miracles in life, that is to say co-create your life. The Law of Deliberate Creation states,

"That which a thought is given to, you begin to attract. What you give thought to with emotion and feelings, you attract more quickly. That which you think about most of the time, you receive."

When you give thought to something you desire with an expectation, belief and emotion in it, you are then ready to receive it. Whatever energy/ vibrations we create (thoughts, feelings, etc.) we receive the same back. This is because everything is connected to everything else. That is why the vibration that you send out by your thoughts, sends ripples and reflects only those vibrations which matches your thought vibrations. The Law of Deliberate Creation is to offer a required vibration knowingly, so that nothing comes into your reality by default. Most of the time, you send out vibrations unknowingly. For example, if you are experiencing something that makes you happy, you are raising your vibration and you will then vibrate happiness. And, if you experience a event that makes you angry or upset, you offer the same negative vibration. The Law of Attraction responds to whatever it is you are vibrating by giving you more of the same and that is why we say Law of Attraction is like a Boomerang.

When the application of the of Law of Deliberate Creation is not there, you are an observer and you create your reality by default. If you focus on your current "reality" whether positive or negative, the Law of Attraction responds to that vibration and you get more of the same. Negative circumstances like fear, worry, doubt, debt etc. the Law of Attraction responds to that negative, feeling and the results in the creation of that the Law of Attraction brings about is more of that negative feeling. Deliberately start focusing on what you do want and send out vibrations that are positive, you are then effectively making use of the Law of Deliberate Creation.

iii. The Law of Sufficiency and Abundance

The world is an abundant place and your natural state is one of abundance and joy. When you are living in abundance, you are connected to the flow of Source Energy. That's the way life is meant to be, you are always connected to the Source Energy. As you go through the process of self transformation, you open yourself to the free flow of energy. Your life becomes abundant. Abundance means plenty and more than you desire i.e. More than Enough of whatever you want. This is not to be confused with having just enough.

You have everything within you right now to live a dream, if you choose to accept that which is your divine birthright.

As a matter of fact, it is a Universe of abundance, although the majority of us have chosen to view it as a Universe of scarcity.

There is an unlimited supply of everything, good and wonderful things, as well as experiences included. There is enough for everyone! We have bought into the lie that there is not enough. This lie is one of scarcity and limitation. 'How can some people have lots and lots of the same thing'. is our Limiting Belief,

The truth is that we are completely abundant, and we are able to create whatever we desire. The truth is that we live in a world where, spiritually and energetically speaking, there is an unlimited supply of goods. You are given life, and have access to the power that you need in order to create your life in any way that you choose. Nothing is taken away out of your "portion" of prosperity if someone else achieves or acquires success. We are eternal beings in physical form; well–being and abundance are the set-points of our 'thermostat', nature has set for our lives on this planet.

Beliefs based on lack/limited quota/short supply, affect our ability to manifest our hearts' desires, from a space of ease and effortlessness. This mentality of lack controls us by keeping our longing for what others have, or fighting to be better than others.

Most of us feel that who we are, what we have, and what we are doing is not enough. You learned about the Law of Attraction. If you feel that nothing is ever enough, that is what you will be attracting into your life. If you feel you are not enough, you are right in your own ways. If you feel what you have is not enough, you will continue to receive not enough.

It is time that we learned to tap into the truth of our being. The truth is that we are more than enough. In this moment, we are perfect, whole and complete just as we are. Because we are growing and evolving beings, we will always desire to have more in our lives, but if we are coming from a place of "not enough" we will never truly feel that whatever we manifest or bring into our lives is enough.

If you are always looking outside of yourself at circumstances and situations to become more than you are, you are not in the now nor appreciating what you have. If you continue to chase things outside of yourself in order to feel that you are enough, you will never feel truly satisfied. There is always more to achieve, acquire, and do. When you come from a place of feeling that everything in your life right now is sufficient, you will know great peace. When you can feel gratitude for what you currently have in your life, while at the same time feel excited for all the things you desire to manifest, you will know complete joy.

If your thoughts are continually focused on lack and limitation, you are asking the Source to give you an abundance of lack and limitation!

1. To express the appreciation /gratitude for what you already have, offer a portion of 5% or more of your time, money and talents unconditionally back into God's work to the world by giving to where you are receiving spiritual knowledge. Experience the magic of tenfold return or more. This is a really important aspect of living abundantly. Every time you freely give money away, you are implying that you are confident that more will come. This is a BIG positive affirmation with a lot of power behind it. Many whom I have had the pleasure of showing the way to use the Law of Attraction, have told me that when they do this, they seem to have more and more – magically. I've seen that the more I give away the more I get back, and the happier and more abundantly I live. It is not

just about getting the money back either. There is such a wonderful, positive feeling that happens when we can give to others. When we can make a contribution to the world, we feel we are living with a purpose and part of the bigger whole world.

2. Create a vacuum so that more good things can flow into your life. Don't fill your life up with things you don't really want. Ask yourself if you want each thing before you buy it. Don't have an abundance of "stuff." Live an abundant life by seeking out the things and experiences that work for you in your core being. Clean out what you are no longer using or need. Clean out closets, desks, etc. Let go of what you no longer want in order to make way for the new. Eliminate drains and waste. Eliminate useless expenditures. Release all thoughts, words, beliefs, and actions that are not abundant. A few weeks ago, I emptied out my parking space by parking my existing car elsewhere, and hey Presto! my decision of buying the new car and delivery of the car happened in just a few days, a wish that was being under consideration for the last few years.

3. Release resistance that interferes with the free–flow of abundance such as resentment, jealousy, envy, self–pity, complaining, criticizing, cruelty, anger, hatred, greed, gluttony, laziness, arrogance, self–centeredness,

lamentation, worry, weakness, competitiveness, fear and doubt. If you are jealous or envious of someone, it implies that what they have is not available for you to have also.

4. Forgive those that have wronged you. When you hold on to your anger, however justifiable it may seem, it only hurts you, not the person with whom you are angry. It also keeps you stuck in the past, rather than going forward into a better present. A great tool to release your anger and let go of any negative feelings is to write a note expressing yourself. Write until you feel you released all your anger inside of you, and then flush it. Forgive those who have taken from you or hurt you. Invest 5 minutes a day in forgiving. "God Bless them All. Thank-You Universe".

5. Allow yourself to be open to receive! Know that you are worthy of abundance from your Source. Being able to receive is healthy, but many people find it difficult. You may need to practice receiving with pure sense of happiness and fulfilment. You may find it difficult at first, but you will get used to it. Think of the pleasure you get in giving out part of whatever you have received. By not receiving generously you are denying other people the pleasure of accepting. It takes one person to give, and the other person to receive. Allow yourself to receive. You deserve abundance! It is your birthright.

6. Take personal responsibility for your life. YOU are the one, 100% responsible for your situations and circumstances. Take total responsibility for all of your finances, health, relationships, career, attitude, thoughts, feelings and actions. Realize there is no "good luck" or "bad luck," there are just conscious and unconscious creators. People who put their faith in "good luck" often spend their lives waiting for things to happen. People who don't believe in luck go out and make things happen. When you take responsibility for your life, you stop playing the victim and stop blaming others for your life experiences. When you blame others, you're stating that you have no control. When you take responsibility, you take control of your own life, and therefore you can make any necessary changes because you are in charge.

We release all our karmas and cleanse our body and Soul by simply uttering these magical phrases to yourself:-

I am Sorry- I do not know what in me co-created this into my Life.

Please Forgive Me- I have absolutely no idea how I created it knowingly or unknowingly.

Thank-You- For taking care of me and solving this for me.

I Love You. - Unconditionally for Everything.

Doing this meditation, will make you feel happier and peaceful.

Meditation of Ho'onopono method.

7. We need to master our inner dialogue because we create our world around us. When you find yourself looking at situations in your life and saying, "There's no good man/woman out there, or I don't have enough money, there are no good jobs for me out there," you should probably also look into your heart and ask, "If there's nothing out there, is there anything in here?" Once you understand that your external reality can't be separated from your internal reality — once you understand that the Universe really is your extended body — it becomes very clear that negative energy within yourself is very self–destructive. Having negative emotions (which stem from your thoughts) is a major barrier to the fulfilment of your desires.

Release resistance so that you can fall back into the flow of well–being and abundance that already exists.

So what are the principles that you live by? Are you ready to recognize the connection between how you are living and the way the Universe works? Are you ready to live in harmony with that connection? Are you ready to put this law into practice?

Then do it Now.

iv. *The Law of Pure Potentiality:-*

The Soul or the Spirit as we call it, is our true self and the essence of our being, is completely untouched by outside conditions, circumstances, or experiences. It does not care who is superior or inferior. It does not compete and compare because everyone is unique and different, yet at the same time, everyone is same and connected. It does not fear any life circumstance, because it only knows love. Criticism does not hurt the soul because the soul always remains untouched, it is eternal.

If you feel you have limitations in life, your ego will feel fear and desire things that will make you feel "free," such as money, prestige, and power. What happens to you when those objects disappear? What if you have all the money you want, and then suddenly it is gone? Your freedom was conditional. Your "power" only lasts as long as the conditions are there.

If you know and develop a relationship with Source, and act "as if" you are part of Source, you will be in touch with pure potentiality. That is why the practice of meditation is so powerful. When you allow yourself to be silent and just "be," you develop a connection with Source, with your Pure Potentiality. You can apply the Law of Pure Potentiality by:

- Talking to Source through sincere genuine prayer.

- Listening to Source through meditation by learning to be still and know that you are one with Source

- Acting like Source – do not judge, do not control, and do not manipulate – simply BE LOVE.

- Thinking, acting, doing, and saying in every conscious moment of choice, "What is in alignment with LOVE?"

- Communing with nature and witnessing the intelligence within every living thing

- Being Non-Judgemental.

Do you know something, in fact, You are Source.

You are connecting to Pure Potentiality when you apply the above mentioned actions. How do you feel when you sit and watch a sunset, or listen to the waves of the ocean crash up against the shore, or smell the beautiful scent of a flower?

Pure Potentiality created all those things, and so much more. You are unlimited, and when you know only love, there is no need to fear, and in the absence of fear, you will know that you are part of Pure Potentiality. Anything is possible, because nothing is impossible. When you are in alignment with the Law of Pure Potentiality, you will feel centred and at peace.

When you know the truth of your being and know who you really are – an extension of Source Energy – you will then know that you are able to fulfil any dream that you have. The more you connect with your true self, and know that you are never separated from it, the more you are in Pure Potentiality.

If you know that you are part of the Universe, and that the Universe will provide all your needs when you require them, then you are unlimited in your potentiality. When you are in alignment with Pure Potentiality, there is no fear. You will be truly free.

v. The Law of Detachment:-

The Law of Detachment states, *"In order to acquire anything in the physical Universe, you have to relinquish your attachment to it."* This does not mean that you have to create by default or that you should not desire or intend for what you want to create. Remember, "meant to be" and "luck" do not exist. We need to work with the Law of Attraction to create what we desire. This again means that the Law of Detachment works in harmony with the Law of Attraction.

When you know that Universe will give you what you need – not necessarily what you want (that's your ego's job) – then you will learn to do the work that is required to be done and move on. The results will take care of themselves. When we trust, i.e. to rely unto Universe, totally, the Universe knows what that perfect timing is, and it happens even faster because we get out of the way. If you stand in the way of the energy creating the outcome, or result, through your doubtfulness, insecurity and fearfulness, you put a barrier in the way and block the efficiency of that flow of energy (resistance). By learning to trust, you live in the wisdom of security and certainty where there are unlimited opportunities being created in the present moment of now. Remember the Law of Pure Potentiality?

Again…see how all the laws work together?

Detachment is another way of saying allowing. It is when you combine your intentions and detach from the outcomes that your desires will manifest.

Detachment comes from having an abundance consciousness, because you trust and know that everything will fall into the perfect place at the perfect time. You know your unlimited potential that you can Be, Do and Have anything in your life. When you are attached to your intentions being a certain way and have perfect pictures, you lose the flow of your creativity and energy. Attachments are resistance and with resistance the Universe cannot deliver your desires to you. The attachments and perfect pictures interfere with the entire creative process.

The Law of Deliberate Creation, the power of intention, and the Law of Detachment all work together to create your desires. Applying the Law of Detachment to your goals and desires allows you to be flexible and to trust when the Universe delivers you something to which you are a vibrational match, but you didn't expect. Detachment allows you to stay open to allow the Universe to bring you, something even better than you thought possible.

When you are in alignment with the Law of Detachment you don't force things to happen, you allow. When you allow, you are in vibrational alignment with pure positive energy and things magically flow to you. This law is about freedom. This law is about relaxing and knowing that every outcome will turn out beautifully if you trust.

So be detached – let go and let Universe – and expect a miracle!

vi. The Law of Polarity:-

This law states that "Unity is plural at a minimum of two." In the duality that exists there are two poles, or opposites, of everything. Polarity represents the two extremes of a "thing" which is abundant at one end and lacks at the other end. For example, temperature has polarity evidenced by hot at one extreme and cold at the other extreme. The temperature "thing" is the same "thing" and it is evidenced by two poles, or opposites, or extremes – hot and cold. Along this same "thing," degrees measure the perception of the attitude of the individual to what is considered hot and what is considered cold. Hot and cold mean different things to different people – so does rich and poor, love and hate, good and bad, etc. What is important in understanding the Law of Polarity is the ability to understand the power of transformation. By choosing to change your perception, your paradigm of someone or something can change from, say, "bad" to "good." This becomes your new reality now. By seeking a higher frequency vibration of energy in this transformation process, the previous lower frequency of vibration of energy gets replaced. "Bad" can become "good," as an example. With the choice made, the decision implemented automatically involves the Law of Attraction – that which is like unto itself is drawn – depending on the choice made in your responses. You can raise your vibrations and positively change others. It is up to you to make a choice to change your perception and your attitude towards something or someone. Just as it is up to you to create the life you desire.

Another example of the Law of Polarity is the physical and the metaphysical. The physical is that which is visible and that which we can see, hear, touch, smell, and taste. The metaphysical is that which we feel, such as emotions, feelings, and energy. In order for you to create what you desire, you have to have both the physical and metaphysical. The physical part of you needs to take action to make things happen in the Universe, while the metaphysical part of you needs to do the energy work. It is when you combine both the polar opposites that we create what we truly desire and achieve a sense of Joy Satisfaction, and Well being

The Law of Polarity was created and exists as a means to enable each of you to explore and experience life to the fullest. A life experience absent of the Law of Polarity would deny you the ability to fully experience/understand your life.

As an example, if lack and limitation did not exist, we would not be able to experience abundance. If failure is known, then success is the other side. The Law of Polarity contains a full spectrum of possibilities ranging from positive to negative and any number of points in between. By developing this understanding and learning to fully accept this concept, you will make an incredible progress in experiencing your ability to mould, shape, and achieve that you consciously desire. Regardless of how you perceive the events, conditions and circumstances of your life, you can learn to understand that everything works together for good.

Regardless of what life experience you may have in your reality right now, you possess the potential, as well as the ability, to experience harmony and fulfilment in each and every area of your life. For every problem there exists its solution and every failure can get converted to success.

You learned with the Law of Attraction that whatever vibration you are sending out through your energy, focus, and attention, whether wanted or unwanted, you attract more of the same back to you. That vibration results in what manifests and is experienced in your life. In order to manifest and experience the events, conditions and circumstances that you perceive as positive, place your predominant focus on that which is positive.

What is extremely important to understand is that within each experience, regardless of how it may be perceived, is the possibility, as well as the ability, to experience the opposite. If you are in debt, within that experience lies the ability to experience financial plenty. If you are currently experiencing difficult and unfulfilling relationships, within that situation lies the possibility of experiencing healthy and harmonious relationships.

In normal condition, we are confused about our desires and only when the adverse condition prevail, the clarity dawns on us about our desires. Once we have that clarity, then we can ask the Universe for what we desire, and we can deliberately create, allow and take action toward our desires. The contrast is realized within every event, condition, situation, or circumstance. For example, when you don't have a partner and feel insecure, you feel that you desire a partner that is secure. It is when you feel financially strapped that you want to be financially free. The potential and possibility to experience the opposite exists. The only things that determine the results we see in our lives are the choices we make on how to perceive something. The only determining factor which lies between these two seemingly opposite circumstances is what you believe to be true and what you choose to focus on.

It is the negative emotions that act as resistance. Resistance happens when we put our focus and attention on what we don't want. When we accept all things for what they are, there is no negative emotion and therefore no resistance. Our desires will manifest with ease and effortlessness. Your contrast can provide you clarity. It is important to quickly take your focus off of what you don't want (contrast) and redirect it onto what you do want (clarity). Like all the Universal Laws, the Law of Polarity exists. It always has and will continue to exist. Regardless of how much your understanding of the law is or ignorance to it, it will continue to exist and operate with exact and precise certainty.

vii. The Law of Reflection:-

The Law of Reflection says that the traits you respond to in others, you recognize in yourself, both positive and negative.

Everything in the Universe is a mirror reflection of YOU. All relationships are a mirror reflection of the relationship with YOU. This includes your relationship with money as well as people in your life. If you have fear or insecurity about money, success, or anyone in your life, then these are reflections of fear and insecurity within your own being. No matter how secure your partner attempts to make you feel or how much money or success you acquire, unless you change your inner feelings of insecurity, you will never feel secure. Have you ever noticed this happens in relationships? One partner is insecure, and no matter what the other partner says or does, that one partner is never secure and questions the love of the other. It is only when you develop self–love with your true self, that you release the feelings of fear or insecurity

First: That which you admire in others, you recognize as existing within yourself. When you notice wonderful qualities in another person, it is because you too have those qualities.

Second: That which you resist and react to strongly in others is sure to be found within yourself.

Third: That which you resist and react to in others is something which you are afraid exists within you. This is the scary part. When we observe this type of quality in another person and have an emotional reaction to it, we certainly don't want to look at it.

Fourth: That which you resist in yourself, you will dislike in others. It is all about self-love. When you realize that you dislike a quality in another person, point the finger back to yourself, and that is a great indication of where you need to develop self-love and self-acceptance.

Understanding the Law of Reflection is a great way to rise above the effect of fear. Fears will always be reflected in your reactions to others. Once you recognize that everything is a mirror reflection of you and your inner world, you can recognize them and change them. As you let go of the fears, you automatically open yourself to express more unconditional love for yourself and others.

Our emotions are a gift from our higher self to let us know how we are feeling in each moment. They are our guidance system. How are you feeling? Remember that feelings are the language of the Soul, and the Soul always stands in its integrity. So how are you really feeling about yourself? Want a clue? What reflections of other people and other things are affecting you? When something irritates you about a person, situation, or circumstance, identify what is really irritating you. Now look deep inside yourself and identify that irritation inside of you.

Conversely, when you are with someone who makes you feel emotionally positive, or you are happy doing an activity, or you see an object you really admire, look deep inside yourself to see what it mirrors to you that you like about yourself. The reflection that you have identified you cannot change in the other person or object. You must change it, if it irritates you, inside of you. If it pleases you, you must enhance it inside of you. You cannot change anyone else – only you. Everything is a reflection if you open your eyes to empowering yourself at the Soul level. Look for the reflections and see what they teach you about you. By wanting to expand your consciousness and choosing to expand your spiritual growth, see the reflections as your continual growth opportunities – see these reflections as fascinating, exciting openings to become Who You Really Are as you strive to remember you are a part of Source.

The Truth and the Law

1. Your outer world of forms and experiences is a reflection of your inner world of thoughts and feelings. As above, so below. As within, so without. That is the Law.

2. The greater your awareness of the presence of Universe within you, the more that presence fills your consciousness. That is the Law.

3. The deeper your understanding of Spirit as the Source, Substance and Activity of your supply, the more permanently that Truth will be etched into your consciousness. That is the Law.

4. It is your spiritual consciousness —your knowledge of the presence of Universe within you as total and complete fulfilment – that interprets itself as every form or experience in your world. That is the Law.

viii. The Law of Forgiveness:-

"In many difficult times it is easy to blame others. Even when it is your fault, it is easy to blame yourself. An attitude that takes your vitality and energy never serves. Learn to forgive. Emotionally let go of a situation and just act to correct it. That is the only way forward."

Bob Proctor

We humans react to the harm or wrong doing of others which is expressed by the emotions created from within. These emotions are the reflections of our feeling that we have been harmed or wronged by something/somebody.

The Law of Forgiveness is aptly explained by a very common phrase of **"Forgive and ye shall be forgiven"**, In nutshell it tells us to put behind the past, and allow the universe to improve our quality of life as per our manifested desires.

If someone hurts you, intentionally or unintentionally, it may or may not be forgotten but can definitely be forgiven to move ahead in the life without the incidence affecting the progress of your life.

The Law of Forgiveness also means you say goodbye to the past. You remember your lessons from it, you remember your past experiences; it is said that if past experiences are good you imagine them so you can smile; and if they're bad, you learn from them. Your life is here and now, it's not there back then.

Forgive yourself for your own honest mistakes, and don't dwell on the bad person you used to be if you used to be such a one. If you have changed, forget about that stranger. At the same time truly and honestly forgive the other person and send blessings to them thereby releasing yourself of those painful thoughts. It makes you feel light and joyful towards every experience in life.

ix. The Law of Gratitude:-

As you express gratitude, it spirals back to you... expanded into multiple forms, Gratitude is the fairest blossom which springs from the soul.

- Henry Ward Beecher

An attitude of gratitude brings great things.

- Yogi Bhajan

Develop an attitude of Gratitude, and give thanks for everything that happens to you, knowing that every step forward is a step toward achieving something bigger and better than your current situation.

- Brian Tracy.

"The whole process of Mental adjustment and Atonement can be summed up in one word 'Gratitude'

Wallace. D. Wattles (The Science of Getting Rich)

"Gratitude is our most direct line to God and the angels If we take the time, no matter how crazy and troubled we feel, we can find something to be thankful for. The more we seek gratitude, the more reason the angels will give us for gratitude and joy to exist in our lives."

- Terry Lynn Tailor.

So what do you understand by the word Gratitude. Gratitude is the vocal expression of acknowledgement, appreciation and gratefulness felt. Expressing Gratitude brings you closer to the Universal vibration level. This helps you to keep in touch with this Source energy, whatever name you call the Universe or GOD.

Expressing Gratitude is a continuous process to be practiced in the life. When you show the Universe that you are already grateful and can appreciate all that it has already given you, and the Universe will deliver manifolds.

When you get up in the morning, the first thing is to be grateful to the universe.

When you start each day with a grateful heart, Light illuminates from within.

"I am grateful for all the Abundance in life. What will be the miracle for today? Today is the most wonderful day of my life. God bless all. Thank-You Universe."

See how miracles happen in your day-to-day life. Do a gratitude walk. Every step say 'Thank-You' to the Universe. Be in the present, be Joyous and Feel the Feeling of Thanking everything and everyone that come across in your life, whether good or bad. As good experiences give Joy, Happiness it increases your vibrations and bad ones teach you something and gives you another opportunity towards Joyful living.

Be grateful for what you already have in your life right now. Focus on the good that is already in your life. It's easy to think about what you don't have, but spend some time each day, thinking about what you do have. Before retiring each day think about 10 things that you are grateful for. When you think of each thing, really FEEL the gratitude within your body and feel your heart opening up and expanding. Everything is energy and when you really use your energy in your body, it is reflected outside of you and is conveyed to Universe.

IV

HUMAN MIND - Limiting Beliefs and Mental Blocks

We discussed about human body and various Koshas earlier. What makes humans vital, living and thriving is the presence of Universe in this body. This presence is called mind. This presence in the form of mind is subdivided in Three (3) parts viz. Conscious mind, Sub-Conscious mind and Deep Sub -Conscious mind.

Conscious mind is responsible for our day to day activities like working, taking decisions, maintaining relations, living in society etc. While functioning in these activities what is used is the various brain capacities like storing memories, recalling them from time to time, analysing the situations and form the reactions, sensory perceptions etc. Also it's important role is to work as an interface to Sub Conscious mind and Deep Sub Conscious mind.

In life based on the day to day experiences, a specific nature of an individual gets created and set. Some of the peculiar Limiting Beliefs and Mental Blocks observed are as follows:

Ego: The conscious state of mind, is always on a run. you have developed and defined yourselves in a particular way and because of this, what you think and act is always right as per your preconditioned mind to act in that certain way. This supposed condition developed is called Ego and your Intellect makes you act, what it thinks is right.

Through exposure to life experiences, you often start believing a certain pattern of vibrations that creates a resistance in receiving that one desires. Although these are absolutely non-serving agents, people defend their continual return to those unpleasant past experiences, situations, events and conclude the patterns as True. The reason behind such beliefs is that, a lot of thoughts and attention are given to those situations and hence the 'truth' is created in a physical, tangible and a definable way.

Culture: You want to do something but its not in your culture to do it. Culture is evolved over the time and people who dare to do different things help culture to evolve.

No time: In day to day life a pattern is set and you are reluctant to deviate. For any new activity in which there is superficial interest a standard excuse that comes up is you do not have time. You are very busy. If something is of higher priority and serious interest in your life, you will make time for it.

I am too old: To undertake a new activity or assignment for which there is no total positive attitude and shaky confidence, you take a stand that you are too old. However that is not true, it's never too late.

If I take my own example, I retired in the year 2010 and I did the Law of Attraction training certification two years ago, I completed my Level-I certification as a practioner for Emotional Freedom Technique (commonly known as EFT or Tapping). I am also now a Certified MahaVastu Expert, from the well respected Vastushastri Dr. Khusdeep Bansal, himself. I am on the way to be a certified Life coach with the team of learned and excellent coaches cum trainers of Christy Whitman's Quantom Success Coaching Academy(QSCA), of the United States. So, if you want to achieve or do something in life, you can do it whenever you start thinking about it and be passionate about it.

Also, Mr. Narendra Modi who got elected as India's Honourable Prime Minister at 64 years, is so energetic and enthusiastic to fulfil his dreams about a new India.

I am too Young: Sometimes you dream of something which involves lot of efforts, innovations hard work apart from living your normal life. Without a serious commitment and priority, you leave alone your dream thinking you are too young. If you look at our young entrepreneur, you will find the young generation has taken over the world by storm. Mr. Rahul Bajaj was the youngest person to take over and successfully handle the giant industrial conglomerate, Mr, Sabeer Bhatia took the world by storm by inventing and making public the concept of e-mail which is the unavoidable part of our life/communication which brought about the 'Third Disruption', the Face Book founder Mark Zukerberg, and the like.

Others: This is a big one and once you have learned to overcome this, you are bound to go places. The others won't let me do this, or what will the others think. Come on you are living your Life, why do you need others to live it for you. Will others eating make you stronger? No!. So forget them all, when it comes to accomplish something in your life. Others are always available to give free advice. Those advices and experiences are never true for any other individual, as every individual has a UNIQUENESS of his own. So simply go by what your intuition, your Heart and passion says.

Never had a chance: Opportunity comes knocking, keep your mind silent to hear that knocking. You don't know, but you never did grab that opportunity since your mind was not calm.

Not good enough: A depressing but a true experience a person has, when he is not so confident about himself. He feels he cannot be successful in his life and whatever he will do.

I don't deserve: Sometimes human mind assumes a low self esteem and decides, you are not a deserving person. you always mess-up with things and tasks.

Born under the wrong stars: You have been told by your elders that when you were born, the stars were not in a favourable position for you to achieve anything and so it's your stars that guide you. You know, you can change your destiny by yourself?

Always bad luck: Your bad luck is very bad. Ha ha. For some it's their luck it seems that guide their life.

V

Expand and Evolve the Universe

So far you have been introduced to basic information about the elements of Universe, Presence of different energies, their inter relationship, known and unknown Universal Laws which are in force that affect our life. Also you are introduced to the concept/science of MahaVastu. Now let us see how all this information can help you to improve the quality of your life and allow you to live and enjoy your dream life. There is scientifically evolved and tested method of fulfilling your desires for ideal life by systematically registering / conveying to the Universe. The Universe has unlimited resources and capabilities to inter-convert various forms of energies.

i - Directions and Placements:-

Let us first understand the exact relation between cause and effect in Nature. A Living or a Built-up Space and the Energies created in the enclosed space affect the Emotions, Intentions and the habitual Thought Process, thereby the sub-conscious mind of the inmates. When placed in a building, these symbols (which are true and ancient friends of human beings) guide the Laws of Universe with a meaning.

They activate the natural Universal powers and unfold and orchestrate special processes that fulfil our desires and goals.

Properly and accurately calculated directions gives a pin-pointed flow of energies and increases the vibration levels for Manifestation of whatever that you Want to be, Do, Happen or Have in your life. In spite of dilution of our sensory power and abilities to decode the Universal messages, we continuously are affected in reality by all Objects and Activities that surround us.

Everything is connected to Everything else. All the Energy fields that are created, on earth or in space are pulsating, creating some effect. They are connected to each and every field on the planet. A spark in a certain field, not only activates that field but also has effect on all other energy fields which are vibrating at the same frequencies.

The Vedic philosophy, from the macro to the micro is best expressed by VastuShastri Dr. Khushdeep Bansal:

"Each person is the centre of the Universe. In him or her are present all the planets, stars, zodiacs, all the five elements and all the forces of nature. What is outside, is exactly what is inside".

The space that we live in is always alive and humming. It acts as if it was an independent Universe in itself. Have you ever noticed that when there is a change of thoughts or moods in the house, the whole space around you either increases your energy levels or decreases depending on the change. Research has been carried out by various scientists like Curry and Hartmann, around the world and have given their conclusions or findings on these energies, which are known as 'Universal Energies'.

When a enclosed space is created for a house, a office, a factory or an industry, a energy gets developed in the centre of the space where the construction is taking place. As the construction progresses different energies are created for different aspects of life for the purpose for which the area is being created. These energies communicate with our mind at it's different levels.

The placing of symbols, paintings, objects (be it 2 Dimensional or 3 Dimensional) in an absolute balanced space, creates an uplifting of vibrations, bringing it in alignment with the Universal vibrations which is said to be vibrating at 432 cycles per second, thereby, you constantly remain in flow or may say so in sync with the Universal energies and get synchronised with the space, thereby making it possible to alter (improve) the condition of one's life. These vibrations directly indicate our emotions and feelings put in the making of the symbol, paintings or sculptures.

We must first be very clear about our Purpose or Intention. Then and only then can we find a effective remedy or a Mantra, which will lead to the manifestation of what we desire.

The Space inside you is an extension of the space around you. Your life is a product of your inner space, do not live a purposeless and directionless life when you can possess true knowledge to liberate you from daily worries and shape your life per your desires.

However, it is mandatory to bring about a balance in the five elements in the liveable space to complete manifestation in your life, your career, relationships or anything that you wish to for that matter. Nature takes its own time and course that is right for you and is far more effective than we can ever imagine.

ii - Science of Programming and Connecting to the Source Energy

In this science of Alchemy of Space, Conscious Mind is believed to have originated from Space; The inner space governs the Inner Mind/Sub Conscious mind. which has the capacity to bring about changes in the outer Space.

There is a continuous interaction between Space and our Subconscious or Deep subconscious mind which takes place at such low frequencies of brain (at around 10 cycles per second) that this communication is imperceptible by our physical (conscious) senses, but of course, it's effects are quite visible in the form of life situations and experiences that we get to face, as well as our reaction or response to them.

The centre of the Human existence is the subconscious mind which conducts and manages the infinite processes of the body, such as blood pressure, heartbeats, to the processes of which we are unaware.

The Miraculous happenings, experiences, the Quantum leaps, occur in the most flowing and subtle manner, as though everything was always around you. This happens when the desires are manifested by the part of our mind which are unknown to us consciously,

The activities of the mind are defined in four levels, measured as cycles per second (cps) known as frequencies of the mind. The four distinct levels of mind are:-

The Conscious Mind:- This is one of the most known level of the mind. Any human being knows that he can think, take decisions, react, respond, feel emotional through the five sensory organs, eyes, ears, nose, tongue and skin, for seeing, hearing, smelling, tasting and touch or feel on the physical level. These are all activities of the Present. This mind operates at a frequency between 21 cps and 14 cps. Known as Beta Level and normally develops and comes into being at the age of 14.

The Sub-Conscious Mind:- The Mind by birth. A free for all, open to any forum, eventuality, experience, environment and absorbs all the energies and emotions dissipated around it since birth. It knows not good or bad, accept or reject, right or wrong. It creates templates of different themes which are impressed and impregnated in the mind. It is the processor or to be more precise 'A Search Engine' of the conscious mind, the monitor. All the decisions, reactions, responses, limiting beliefs, mental blockages, good or bad emotions, feelings are a result of the imprinted templates that are getting embossed in it every moment of one's life. This mind when operating between 14 cps and 7 cps is said to be in the Alpha Level and at this level, it can be brought to the best use by mankind. This mind and the other minds only understand the language of Vibrations. This is how our Emotional Guidance system comes to our rescue letting us know, whether we are on the right path (Feeling Good) or the wrong path (Feeling Bad).

The Deep Sub-Conscious Mind:- This is a Deep sleep level and operates at frequencies between 7 cps and 4 cps and is known as the Theta level. At this level one is able to reach required solutions, help in the healing of self and others and also bring about a change in the embedded code by birth thereby being capable of changing even one's Destiny.

The Super Conscious Mind:- This is the highest state of mind operating between 4 cps and near zero cps and connects one, to one's Higher Self, Soul Energy, Angel, Teacher or whatever name one may call. A person whilst sleeping dips to this frequency four times in the night and that can be seen when the person awakens in a fresh mood, otherwise, he would feel tired or lack of sleep. This level is known as the Delta level, it's the level of Ultimate or Absolute bliss, when one remains constantly at this Delta level.

Disclaimer: All the higher states of mind can be achieved by meditation and other processes, to scientifically and spiritually bring down the frequencies. The person must be brought back to his original state of mind in a proper guided manner. Never ever force someone to a lower frequency as it will put the person at a risk of going into Coma.

The simpler way of getting connected with the Universe to bring about the desired changes is by activation of the Law of Attraction and the Law of Deliberate Creation, and become a co-creator yourself, you can do it in three different ways:-

i) Ask- With a directed energy increase your vibration levels. The Universe understands only one language directly, apart from Sanskrit and Hebrew, and that is Vibration and it always says one thing, *"Your Wish Is My Command"*.

So, put in all your 'Feeling Good' emotions at every moment of your life.

"You can begin right now to Feel Healthy, You can begin to Feel Prosperous, you can begin to Feel the Love that's surrounding you, even if it is not there, And what will happen is The Universe will correspond to the nature of that inner song, the universe will correspond to the nature of that inner feeling, and MANIFEST, because that's the way you FEEL."

-Dr. Michael Beckwith.
(The Secret).

ii) *Believe* – Believe that it is coming to you, do not worry about How. The HOW is not your Domain. In one of the most authentic Indian scriptures," The Bhagwad Gita", Lord Krishna says, "It is in your domain to take Inspired action on whatever that is your spark of a thought, the result is bound to follow. The result, however, is not your domain. I am responsible for the result, you simply take the desired /inspired action."

"You do not How, it will be shown to you."
                                              - Bob Proctor.(The Secret).

However, if you dwell on the result all the while, it will get destroyed and will never come to you. As it was shown in the Cycle of Balance, eg., Fire is doused by Water, so in the cycle of creation it says that Water creates Air/Wood, Air/ Wood creates Fire. So the spark in you (Water) gives that inspired thought to take action(Air/Wood) and the result that follows is Fire. So if you directly follow the result i.e Water to Fire it is doused and destroyed. Nothing ever would happen for you.

iii) *Visualise*

Visualise your desires in 3D or 2D, give it colour and sound and feel the feelings of having achieved them. Then "Let Go and God."

"Assume the Feelings of the Wish Fulfilled"

-Neville Goddard.

iv) *Receive* - When we have Asked for something and have the Belief it will come to you, then the Mind which has first received the information starts searching the desired information. With whichever space we are connected, the Mind also gets connected to that Space. Be ready to receive. Be in the allowing mode, no resistance exists in that mode. Be in sync with the universal vibration, (It has been scientifically seen that the universe vibrates at a frequency of 432 cycles per second.) that is when the Manifestation takes place.

iii - Manifestation

Before we proceed towards the actual processes of manifestation, let us understand what manifestation means in our day-to-day life.

Manifestation is registering a life situation, experience, physical needs such as Money, a New Car, New House and the like, by using the different natural laws of the universe for co-creating all that you need to Be, Do, Have and Happen in your present moment or a future reality, which is termed as Miracles of our day-to-day life. This deliberate creation of Miracles is called Co-creation.

Water is one of the five elements in the universe which is responsible for creation. The 'flowing' property of water is what sets into motion the Spark within you to activate the Attraction process, which begins from our fifth layer of existence. The zone of the self-illuminating Manifester or 'Budhdhar' the name of the power because of which this Universe came into existence who is responsible for manifesting our goals/desires and it's energy has maximum potential towards the North zone of the space where we are in, at the time of manifesting.

The Human consciousness gets affected by self-illuminating powers and also the negative powers working within you at every moment of one's life.

Any spark or desire is a self- illuminating power, however immediately there is a thought of doubt, fear, your deservedness and your limiting beliefs govern the negative powers in the enclosed space where these energies get created. The 45 Universal energies that work and govern you, once you are able to bring these energies in the flowing mode or a favourable mode, success, prosperity, wealth and happiness will start accruing naturally in the most subtlest manner.

In life there are 3(Three) time zones, viz. Past, Present and Future. Past can't be altered, however future can be altered by manifesting your desire in current present. In short, the seeds of desires coming true in current present, are sowed in the past.

In Manifestation, your desires of the of the conscious mind are conveyed and registered to deep sub-conscious mind which is connected with the Universe. Thus Universe expands and evolves to fulfil your desires to the satisfaction of your conscious mind.

Manifestation is registering for "Bringing into Reality" one's thoughts, that have been activated by an individual, by continuously focussing on it without losing sight, but not just concentrating on the Final outcome. You do so for a period of 68 seconds continuously, till it finally activates the Law of Attraction, and being in resonance of the thought, thereby being in the receiving mode. Be Grateful and Thank the Universe for having realised the thought so that one is into a state of Allowing, and the universe will rearrange and unfold all that it needs to, to Manifest whatever it is that your desire is. The procedure involved in the process of Manifestation is as mentioned below.

1. Write down five things you want to manifest in your life at this point of time. Once done write five more.

2. *Now put your hand on the heart and read your goal /
    Desire, note the energy level within you on a scale of*

0 to 10. 0 being 'No energy' and 10 being 'Maximum Energy'. Here we are talking about good emotions, because 'Feeling Good' is what takes to your higher self.

3. *Take the goal/desire which gives you the maximum raise in energy or vibration.*

4. *Write down on a fresh page, your goal/desire having the highest level of emotion. Divide the page by a vertical line.*

5. *On the left hand side write-Contrast with respect to your goal above write all that you feel are the hindrances, limiting beliefs, pre-conditioning that exists, one after another.*

6. *On the right hand side, write the positive of the statement written against the one on the left and then strike-off that negative statement on the left side.*

On completing this you will be ready to write your goal in a structured manner as under:-

"I am in the process of attracting all that I need to Be, Do Know and Have, to attract my Ideal Desire."

In the body of the statement, write the positive statements on the right hand column by prefixing phrases like," I now Choose to ....this or Something Better "and the like.

Complete it with this closing statement:-

"The Law of Attraction is Unfolding and Orchestrating all that needs to happen to bring about my Ideal desire."

Always be Grateful to the universe for everything you have got at this Moment.

Now, take a stop-watch and for exactly 68 seconds think, speak or read your goal/passion

The first 17 seconds activates your thought, which grows 10 times stronger every 17 seconds and at the end of 68 seconds that strengthened thought full of emotions and feelings activates the Law of Attraction.

Thank the Universe.

Inspired Action:-

Now that you have placed your order in the catalogue of the universe, the universe always says **"Your Wish Is My Command".** The process of attraction starts and the universe sends out signals to tune to the frequency you are resonating at and shows signs by way of news, paper ads, TV shows, signboards, dreams, intuitions, flashes, whatever way it feels appropriate. Your job is to take inspired action in response to the signs shown by the universe. These actions will then make the universe to unfold and orchestrate to bring about whatever that is your desire.

Now you have read and understood the working of the Universal laws and the method of Manifestation. Practicing one of the following before Manifesting any desire will result in accelerated effects.

1. Do a five minute deep breathing exercise and watch the flow of your breaths during Inhaling and Exhaling and see the calming of your mind, bringing down the frequency of your brain.

2. If you want to instead meditate, use this link to bring about yourself into a state of deep level of the sub-conscious mind.

VI

CO-CREATION EFFECT
OF MAHAVASTU

We begin this with the most important and sought after desire.

Money matters

This is a big one. Everyone wants Money. Money is an essential commodity of life, it's an 'energy' that changes hand and in turn gives you something that you need or want. An abundance of money is what one expects.

But do you have that feeling of abundance?

Isn't this what most of us think?
We have to work hard for money
Money is the root cause of all evil

We can't afford it

Rich people are criminals

Rich people are Greedy

Not everyone can be rich

I don't care about money

You can't be rich and spiritual.

Learn to bring about:-

Awareness

Understanding

Change in Your Thoughts

Observe your Thoughts & Actions

Say this everyday "I am so Happy and Grateful, now that I have more than enough money coming in from Multiple Sources in regular intervals and in increasing amounts."

Place the lord of Wealth and Gaurdian of Treasures of the Universe in Zone I. This Lord is known as Kuberji, is three-legged, has eight teeth and large, round and protruding eyes. He is pot-bellied always smiling and happy. Alternatively you can even place the Happy Buddha to have a similar effect for your manifestation.

In addition to the above, Be in the PRESENT instead of being in the Past. Ask yourself: What will you do with money? Write the cheque of the Bank of Universe on your name for the total amount that you would like to receive every month!

> The cheque can be for choice
> of your currency
> The date should be today's date!
> Sign the cheque & place on your work desk

UNIVERSAL BANK (UN)LIMITED	DATE____ / ____ / ____	
PAY_____	Rs.	
Rupees_____		
_____		
Drawer Account: Unlimited Abundance		

⑈ᑫᑫ00222⑈   221ᑫᑫ0022⑈:   222ᑫᑫᑫ⑈ 00   THE UNIVERSE

Disclaimer: This is not an instrument to be used with any bank. Visit us at: www.goldeninspiration.com

NOTE: It's important to fill in only that amount you emotionally feel comfortable with. Do not write an amount which you yourself will ridicule.

Bless all whom you feel and believe are bad, criminals not worth having all that money. This action of blessing all will change your attitude and feelings towards the pre existing beliefs and mindset about money and moneyed people.

Try this exercise, simply drop a currency note in a place where it will be of some use to someone. What were your feelings while dropping it, what was the emotion attached to that currency note. If it was positive, you have cleared all the barricades of having more than enough money. You can now use money at your will at whatever be the amount that needs to be spent.

Very Important:-Do this exercise without expecting back anything. Just Bless whosoever gets that money and don't look back to see who got it.

The below mentioned is one of the best ways to utilise whatever be your monthly or Annual Income.

> 5% to Charity
> 10% on self requirements/welfare
> 20% set aside for future use
> 65% for current expenses

Health

How you can come out of growing negative thoughts of one's health.

Repeat the phrases as below during the day, whenever you feel drained out due to health worries:-

Let us say to ourselves:-

a) I have a perfectly healthy body and mind.

b) I am feeling young, full of energy and vitality.

c) I am loving every cell of my body.

If possible, try & keep your medicines in zone II

Spiritual Aptitude

Spirituality is something which everyone knows that needs to be followed. However, some have faith and belief and some hold a different opinion. Those who believe go further into practising it and try to take themselves higher into the mist of ultimate bliss.

They perform their regular prayers, meditate and follow the path of Godliness and serve humanity for their upliftment.

Clear all physical clutter and perform your spiritual duties in zone III.

Relationship

Relationships can be good or stressed depending on how you respond or react to a situation with your relations, be it with spouse, parents, elders, children, relatives or friends and try to maintain balance in your relationships.

Place your family photograph in happy times or a metallic white coloured pair of white love birds or to increase your skills place your ancestral photos or instruments/tools of your skills in zone XI.

Career

A Career in a job, promotions and going higher in the corporate ladder. A Career in your Business, Expand, Diversify, go global, invent new things, create jobs for skilled and needy people, be a part in growing of your country, and of course make more and more money.

Professionals would like to increase their creative aptitude by using their knowledge, their learned and adapted skills.

Performers would like to show their talents by their performances, spread their culture to the world, build appreciating audiences and reach a state of Peak performance thereby taking their audiences to higher state of mind.

Place a pair of red horses in Zone IX.

Education

Gaining knowledge and educating oneself is a very important aspect of life. By education we not only mean getting degrees or diplomas, but also learning how to live a life and help others live their lives by showing them the path to gaining knowledge.

With the help of knowledge from books and life experiences, we manage the available resources that lead us to living a gainful life. Educate ourselves, our children, our siblings and all who you can, to improve their life and lifestyle and elevate them in the society around them.

Your sub-conscious mind can be programmed to achieve these levels of education by placing whatever that imparts knowledge to oneself in the zone XII.

Support

Man is a social animal as it is said. So everyone depends on everyone else. Whether it is money, relationship, career, spiritual growth, health, education, political career, joy, Happiness, you name it and it requires some support. Like for money support of your job, business, banks, government and so on.

For Relationship support of your parents, spouse, children, relatives, neighbours and many more.

For Career it is your educational skills, your teachers, trainers, your boss, your employees, your colleagues, subordinates.

For Spiritual Growth support or blessing of a Guru, a Spiritual teacher some spiritual books or Mantras.

For health it could be the medical practitioner, a physical training expert, a yoga teacher or a Meditation teacher.

For a political career it is the support of the masses, the ruling party or the party you wish to follow and so on and so forth.

Programme your mind by placing relevant objects for support you want in Zone XIV.

To Conclude:-

For leading desired and successful life,

- you ask not from divine providence, for more riches but more wisdom, with which to accept and to use wisely, the riches you received at birth in the form of power to control and direct your mind to whatever ends you desire.

- you can employ and use Universal Laws of Co-creation, Solutions of MahaVastu OR both.

Manifest whatever it is you desire, with an Intention to

'Evolve and Expand our Ever-Expanding Universe.'

'Tathatsu'

(It's a Sanskrit word, God's/Universe's way of saying,' It shall be so, as you hope/wish')

REFERENCES

1) MahaVastu - 2011,

2) MahaVastu Remedies - 2012

3) The Alchemy of Inner Mind - 2012

   - by VastuShastri Khushdeep Bansalji, Founder of MahaVastu.

   www.mahavastu.com

4) The teachings by Golden Inspirations, Delhi, India.

   www.goldeninspiration.com

5) Contents from The Seven Universal Laws- Christy Whitman's coaching academy, QSCA., USA.

   www.qsca.com

6) Jerry and Ester Hicks- Ask and it's Given.

   www.abraham-hicks.com

7) Inspiration from "The Secret" by Rhonda Bryne.

   www.thesecret.tv

GLOSSARY

1) Gayatri Mantra

A prayer of praise that awakens the vital energies and gives liberation and deliverance from ignorance.

2) The Seven Main Chakras

The seven fundamental chakras are known as _muladhara_, which is located at the perineum, the space between the anal outlet and the genital organ; _swadhisthana_, which is just above the genital organ; _manipuraka_, which is just below the navel; _anahata_, which is just beneath where the rib cage meets; _vishuddhi_, which is at the pit of the throat; _ajna_, which is between the eyebrows; and _sahasrara_, also known as _brahmarandra_, which is at the top of the head, where when a child is born, there is a soft spot.

3) Brahma, Vishnu, Mahesh

Within the Hindu Trinity of Brahma, Vishnu and Mahesh, Brahma is the Creator-Vishnu -the Preserver and Mahesh-the Destroyer. Nevertheless, Brahma grew in a lotus out of the navel of the sleeping Vishnu. The daily alteration of light and dark is attributed to the activity of Brahma.

4) Physics

It is the natural science that involves the study of matter and its motion through space and time, along with related concepts such as energy and force. More broadly, it is the general analysis of nature, conducted in order to understand how the universe behaves.

Quantum Physics:- This is theoretical basis of modern physics that explains the nature and behaviour of matter and energy on the atomic and sub-atomic level.

Meta Physics:- It is a branch of Philosophy that studies the relationship between mind and matter. Often used to describe things that lack the 'facts'.

5) Karma

Means action, work or deed; it also refers to the spiritual principle of cause and effect where intent and actions of an individual (cause) influence the future of that individual (effect). Good intent and good deed contribute to good karma and future happiness, while bad intent and bad deed contribute to bad karma and future suffering. Karma is closely associated with the idea of rebirth in some schools of Asian religions. In these schools, karma in the present affects one's future in the current life, as well as the nature and quality of future lives.

6) Ho'onopono Method

Ihaleakala Hew Len, co-authored a book with Joe Vitale called *Zero Limits* referring to Simeona's ho'oponopono teachings. the main objective of ho'oponopono is getting to "the state of Zero, where we would have zero limits. No memories. No identity." To reach this state, which Len called 'Self-I-Dentity', one has to repeat constantly, according to Joe Vitale's interpretation, the mantra, "I love you. I'm sorry. Please forgive me. Thank you." It is based on Len's idea of 100% responsibility, taking responsibility for everyone's actions not only for one's own. If one would take complete responsibility for one's life, then everything one sees, hears, tastes, touches, or in any way experiences would be one's responsibility because it is in one's life. The problem would not be with our external reality, it would be with ourselves. To change our reality, we would have to change ourselves. Total Responsibility, according to Hew Len, advocates that everything exists as a projection from inside the human being. the reality of the consciousness of others. Instead, it views all consciousness as part of the whole, any error that a person clears in their own consciousness should be cleared for everyone.

7) Emotion

A mental state that arises spontaenously rather than through conscious effort and is often accompanied by physiological changes, a feeling the emotions of Joy, sorrow, and anger.

8) Devs and Asuras

In Hindu cosmology the Asuras (Demons) enjoy the same status as the Devas(Gods) and Humans. The Gods, Demons and Humans are considered children of Brahma. They all practise the same dharma and worship the same Trimurthis (Trinity), but differently. Brahma provided them with the same knowledge. However, because of difference in attitude, understanding and thinking, each understand the same knowledge in different ways.

Truth is the same for all. Because of the difference in our temperament and thinking, we receive it differently.

The devas operate at the mental and intelligence level. Since they possess a lot of intelligence and analytical ability, they are not easily impressed by the surface reality. Hence they can clearly distinguish between reality and illusion.

9) Kuberji

He is the Lord of Riches and Treasures in Hinduism pantheon of Gods and Goddesses.

ABOUT THE AUTHOR

The author of this book, Sunil Chhaya, is a qualified Electrical Engineer, a Chartered Engineer and a Fellow of the Institution of Valuers (Plant and Machinery) and had served AIR-INDIA LTD. for a little above three decades, retiring as a General Manager.

A Certified trainer of Law of Attraction and a Certified expert in the field of scientifically analysing and suggesting fruitful remedies based on a very ancient Indian science, which is now known as MahaVastu. He is a person with a spiritual bend of mind and has studied and Certified himself for Alternate Healing Techniques.

After his retirement five years ago, he made it his purpose of life to share the knowledge to expand and evolve the universe, to his fellow human beings. This passion of assisting our Universe in it's ongoing process of evolution, brought him the thought of going a step further and sharing his knowledge to a larger number of people in a quicker, simple and easily adoptable method, by putting into words his call to "Join hands to Expand and Evolve the Universe" this book which he names:-

"The Science of Co-Creation".
A Maha Way to Manifest Your Desires

Printed in the United States
by Baker & Taylor Publisher Services